GW01043804

To Kate, bestest friend – thanks for being determined to endure the pain of 60 miles with me and for making my birthday (all 5 days of it) special!

love x

THE RUTLAND ROUND

by John Williams

Enjoy Walking in Rutland.

John Williams

Maps by Jeff Nightingale.

Published by CPRE Rutland.

ISBN 1 871890 44 6

RRP £6

Printed by BJ's, Stamford, Lincs PE9 1XP

THE RUTLAND ROUND

by John Williams

The Sections

		Miles	Total Distance
1	Oakham to Uppingham	13	13
2	Uppingham to Barrowden	$12^{1}/_{4}$	$25^{1}/_{4}$
3	Barrowden to Empingham	$13^{1}/_{4}$	$38^{1}/_{2}$
4	Empingham to Thistleton	$13^{1}/_{2}$	52
5	Thistleton to Oakham	$12^{3}/_{4}$	$64^{3}/_{4}$

The Rutland Round was devised by John Williams, Rights of Way Officer for C.P.R.E. Rutland with the co-operation of Rutland County Council. It was officially opened on 12th April 2000 by Air Chief Marshall Sir Jock Kennedy, the then Lord Lieutenant of Rutland. Finance for specific waymarking of the route and production of the first edition of the guide was achieved by a Lottery grant.

Assistance in initially surveying the route was given by Rutland Ramblers and The Rutland & Harringworth Chowder & Marching Society, the latter having walked the complete Round during the summer of 1998.

The logo was designed by Helen Archer. Geoff Frowde assisted with the historical matter in the guide book.

This second, up-dated, edition has been made possible by a grant from CPRE.

CPRE are committed to protecting hedgerows and dry stone walls, features which give beauty and character to rural landscapes and are valuable habitats for wildlife. Their patterns stitch the characteristic patchwork quilt over the countryside and they are intimately connected with our history and ancestors. We ask walkers, who we know value the counryside, to give thought to helping us to survey hedgerows by considering joining CPRE. Your subscription would help us to carry out this work. Even better, by being active as a member of your local branch and assisting with actual surveys you would help to ensure the survival of the rural landscape for future generations. Details of how to join CPRE can be found at the end of this book.

Photographs have been provided by Richard Adams, Graham Dunn and the author.

The line-drawing of the Bishop's Eye at Lyddington is by Ray Eden.

The Rutland Round is a circular walk of about 65 miles round the County of Rutland. This guide breaks the walk into five, near-equal sections and travels in an anti-clockwise direction, but it can be started at any point and walked in either direction. The walk always remains inside the County of Rutland although along the northern section between Thistleton and Teigh the path is actually the boundary where one foot may occasionally stray into Leicestershire. The route follows near the perimeter of the county but deliberate diversions are made to visit Rutland Water and the County Town of Oakham.

The route is waymarked with the acorn device set in a yellow arrow placed on a dark green background. Latterly a blue arrow has been introduced on replacement signs on bridleways. The complete sign is used at all junctions with roads and other paths. On long paths either the full sign or the central acorn device is repeated at intervals to reassure that the correct route is being followed.

Maps are provided in this guide but it is recommended that either the 1: 50,000 or the 1: 25,000 Ordnance Survey maps are used in conjunction with them.

There are suitable places to park cars at all these suggested starting points. In Oakham these are Pay and Display Parks. (no charge on Sundays or Bank Holidays.

General Information

Always follow the Country Code.
Enjoy the countryside and respect its life and work
Guard against all risk of fire
Fasten all gates
Keep your dogs under close control
Keep to public paths across farmland
Use gates and stiles to cross fences, hedges and walls
Leave livestock, crops and machinery alone
Take your litter home
Help to keep all water clean
Protect wildlife, plants and trees.
Take special care on country roads
Make no unnecessary noise

Remember, as a general rule, when walking on roads with no pavement to walk on the right-hand side facing oncoming traffic.

Useful Maps:–
Landranger (1:50,000) 130 & 141
Explorer (1:25,000) 234 & 247

Further copies of this book can be obtained by post from
Rutland Water Tourist Information Centre, Sykes Lane, Empingham, Oakham, Rutland. LE 15 8PX

The price will be £6.00 plus p&p. Cheques need to be made payable to:- Anglian Water.
Telephone 01780 686800 before ordering to find the current price of p&p.

The walk instructions are printed in Times New Roman type.

The Historical data is in italic script.

Suggested possible diversions to points of interest are given in blue Eras type.

Approaching Braunston from the South in Winter.   R.Adams

Dovecote at Brooke Priory. R.Adams

OAKHAM TO UPPINGHAM

There are a number of Pay and Display car parks in Oakham.

Leaving Oakham the route visits Egleton at the head of Rutland Water then continues to Brooke and on to Braunston. From there it crosses the area of the old forest of Leighfield (Pronounced LIE-FIELD) and on to Belton-in-Rutland. It continues to Wardley and then Uppingham.

	Miles	Total Distance
Oakham to Egleton	$1^1/_4$	$1^1/_4$
Egleton to Brooke	$2^1/_2$	$3^3/_4$
Brooke to Braunston	$1^1/_4$	5
Braunston to Belton	$3^3/_4$	$8^3/_4$
Belton to Wardley	$1^1/_4$	10
Wardley to Uppingham	3	13

SK Start from the Rutland County Museum, Map ref. (863085)
Opposite the Rutland Museum is Catmose, the Offices of Rutland County Council. Turn right and leave Oakham by the Uppingham Road (A6003). Proceed along the road and cross the stream at Swooning Bridge.

So named it is said because from here you could see the gallows at the top of the hill in front at Mount Pleasant, the point where your path leaves the road.

As you make your way to the edge of the town a field path leaves the road on the left hand side.
Crossing diagonally to a gate in the right hand hedge, pass through it and turn left along the hedge, then bear right crossfield and reach the Oakham bypass.
Cross this and follow the path to Egleton
Ahead there are views of Rutland Water.

Just out of reach of Rutland Water which flooded the area in the 1970's, Egleton has an interesting church with some Norman work dating from 1160. Note the remarkable South doorway and 15th. century chancel screen. The Finch family of Burley-on-the-Hill once owned the village and you can get some good views of the Burley great hall. It was Daniel Finch, 2nd. Earl of Nottingham who built the present house between 1694 and 1708. There is an inscription on the old school house in Egleton which refers to the family. A new Anglian Water Birdwatching Centre of international importance has been established at Egleton with a 450 acre nature reserve incorporating eleven hides overlooking lagoons and further views over the western shores of Rutland Water. During 2010 further lagoons are being completed to ensure satisfactory habitat is maintained for the birds when the additional equipment at Wing water treatment works will cause greater variation in the water level of the reservoir.

When you reach the road the parish church of St. Edmund's is just to your left. Turn right and make your way along Church Road. On reaching the end of the village turn right and continue up the road towards the A6003 leaving the

A 606

Oakham

SWOONING BRIDGE

Small gate

Brooke Covert East

A6003

Egleton

BIRDWATCHING CENTRE

entrance to the Bird Watching Centre behind you. Cross the A6003 and the railway line and, with the hedge on your left, take the path up the hill in front. At the second gateway make for the right-hand hedge at the point that the second large tree is, then follow the hedge to reach a gate into a track. Continue along this track

Braunston

Blue Ball P.H.

R. GWASH

Prior's Coppice

past the wood (Brooke Covert East) on your right until the track bears right. Here take the marked route left through the gateway. The Macmillan Way is also waymarked here. Follow this to Brooke entering by Bridge Farm. Continue to the church and carry on through Brooke taking the road towards Braunston.

Not much remains of the lovely, secluded village of Brooke but the church is unique and well worth visiting. Rutland church-building was said to be best between 1150 and 1350 and anyway had ended by 1540. But this church was in a terrible state by 1577 when the archdeacon's visitation showed the chancel in ruins and the curate 'marvellously overcome with drink'. It was accordingly almost entirely rebuilt in 1579 and little has altered since. Look for wooden box pews with 17th. century graffiti in the chancel.

Where the road bends sharp right go through the gap into the grassed area in front of you. The path continues just off

the road past farm buildings until crossing a stile into a field and then along the hedge until you come to the fieldgate near Brooke Priory.

Brooke Priory, a fine red-brick house of the late 17th. Century on the site of the 12th Century priory of which nothing remains. The Noel family who acquired the site in 1549 also built a house there but only the porter's lodge (now a dovecote) and a ruined gateway are still there.

Staying in the field, follow the tractor-track to the left and on round the field edge. Turn right at a waymark post and cross the

BROOKE PRIORY

BRIDGE FARM

Brooke

stream at the footbridge. Over a stile come to the bridleway. Cross straight over the bridleway and, taking the stile by the gateway opposite, follow the path diagonally to the left-hand hedge. Here cross a stile, turn right and go to the corner of the field. Now, with the River Gwash to your right, continue into the next field by crossing over a stile alongside a horse¬-jump. Head for the gate in the opposite hedge. Go through and across the next field to a stile about 30yds to the right of the field-gate.

River Gwash at Braunston.   R.Adams

Over this do not go towards the gap in the hedge straight across the field but walk towards the right-hand hedge and leave by a stile in the far right corner. A passageway takes you into Braunston village, entering by "Panter's Lane". Your way lies left but you may wish to deviate slightly to the right where you can then see the "Blue Ball Inn". Opposite is All Saints Church.

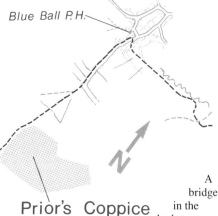

Braunston

Blue Ball P.H.

This attractive ironstone church has an outsize clock mounted on the tower. Inside are traces of medieval wall paintings and outside is a pagan idol below the west tower. There are many interesting old cottages of local ironstone and farmhouses such as Cheseldyne Farm (1604).

Prior's Coppice

Leigh Lodge

To continue from Panter's Lane turn left and take the road, Wood Lane, out of the village until, at the top of the hill, where it takes a left-hand bend, carry on straight ahead into the lane passing the farm buildings to take the fieldpath on the left. You are now also following the Leighfield and Macmillan Ways to Belton. The path crosses straight over the field and down to the hedgerow.

A bridge in the hedge crosses a small stream. The path continues across the field to a stile by a gateway and on to the corner of the woodland. Here it carries on along a broad grassed track at the edge of the field with the wood, Prior's Coppice, on the left. In the field to your right two lakes have been constructed. *Prior's Coppice, one of the few intact remnants of the Royal Forest of Leighfield which once covered the western half of the County of Rutland, is now a nature reserve and well worth a visit, particularly when the bluebells are out. The square shaped villages of Braunston and Belton are tell-tale evidence of old enclosures within the forest - where houses surrounded an open space and where animals could be driven for protection and security.*

There are a number of paths through the coppice. To enter it make your way in from the southern boundary.

Your route lies to the south following the waymarked path over the stile ahead, keeping the hedge on the right to the next field boundary where, after passing a small plantation, it turns S.E. over a stile and crosses the field diagonally downhill to Leigh Lodge. Here another stile takes you onto a track **[If there is a crop such as rape covering the**

Alongside Prior's Coppice.

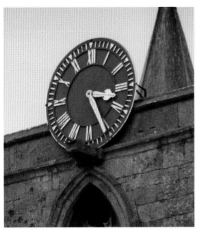

Braunston Church with oversize clock.

Should you decide to do this, turn right towards the church and follow the road. The Sun Inn will be in front of you. On leaving the Sun, with your back to the pub, turn right outside the doorway and continue to join the road taking you out of the

Prior's Coppice

Leigh Lodge

path it is possible to continue down the track to the bottom of the field and turn left.]

Farm buildings

Belton

Sun P.H.

Lime Tree

Wardley

A47

Wardley Wood

village by the small green with the seat under the lime tree.

Belton contains a number of good houses from the 16th. and 17th. centuries including a fine manor house built by the Haselwoods. The family bought the manor in 1557 and kept a large household there. On the house opposite the Sun is a plaque commemorating the 2nd. April 1982 when Belton was renamed Belton-in-Rutland in the presence of the Duke of Rutland and Mr. Kenneth Lewis MP.

As you are leaving the village, just below the small green with a seat under a lime tree, there is a path on the left-hand side. Start through a gateway and almost

A47

Leicester Rd.

CASTLE HILL Motte & Bailey

Uppingham

Here, keeping the building on your right, turn downhill to follow the broad tarmac track until, in just under a mile and after climbing an incline, it meets a stony surfaced track by some farm buildings. Turn left and, after about 50 yards, turn right down a rough bridleway. This will eventually join a tarmac road which leads on to Belton-in-Rutland.

Keep to the left at all junctions at Belton, unless you are visiting the Sun Inn.

immediately branch right through a second gate.

Cross the field to a stile in the far right-hand corner, go over this stile and keep along the left-hand hedge looking for a bridge over the stream. Cross over this bridge and go to your right parallel with the hedge until you come to the next stile. Cross this, bear left and follow the waymarks to the old A47 making sure you have the hedge on your right after you cross the bridleway. Go down steeply, cross over a bridge and up to a stile. Then go through the hedge in front joining the old A47. Turn left then right on the tarmac road, continuing until you reach the present A47 on Wardley Hill. Cross the main road and directly opposite is the way into Wardley Village.

From the corner by Wardley church take the track slightly to the right. This looks like the drive to a house but is a track through the fields to the woods and on. Follow this until the woods are on your left. Shortly a track leads off left into the wood. This leads up hill and can be wet. Continue to the crest of the hill and down to a clearing. Turn left and after about 50yds.. turn right onto a hard surfaced track. Leave this track very soon as it swings left and follow the waymarked, green track straight ahead. This again can be wet. Keep on this track to the edge of the woodland. Pass through the gate and cross the field keeping midway between the woods on either side. Go through the gate and continue across the field to find a bridge and gate into the final field. Continue following the track up the slope to join the Leicester Road into Uppingham.

Turn right and make your way into Uppingham. At the junction of Leicester Road and North Street West take the No Entry' road on the right. Continue on past the Exeter Arms on your right, to the junction of High Street West and Stockerston Road.

If you wish to spend time in Uppingham turn left and make your way into the town.

Otherwise turn right along Stockerston Road.

Uppingham is a gem of a small market town whose High Street shows a glittering selection of architectural styles from 16th. to 20th. century. It has had a market since 13th. Century. The church (tower late 14th. Century) was considerably reconstructed in 1861. Perhaps the chief object of interest is the pulpit from which Jeremy Taylor preached as rector (1637 - 42), later chaplain to Charles I during the Civil War. The independent school occupies much of the town and owns some fine buildings. Its Elizabethan schoolroom dates from 1584.

Morris Dancers in Uppingham Market Square.

"Bishop's Eye", Lyddington.

Ray Eden

UPPINGHAM TO BARROWDEN

There is plenty of parking in the centre of Uppingham. If you are only leaving one or two cars it is possible to find space in turnings off the Stockerston road nearer the point where the footpath leaves the road.

From Uppingham the route follows fieldpaths along the crest of the ridge until, at Beaumont Chase, you are faced with magnificent views over the valley before you. Here you turn and, keeping to the higher ground, make your way past Stoke Wood and views of The Eyebrook Reservoir eventually going down to Stoke Dry. From here the route continues to Lyddington on to Seaton then Morcott and finally to Barrowden.

A part of Uppingham School.   R.Adams

the right. Follow this diagonally across the first two fields then, after crossing stiles and a bridge, carry on diagonally right to the corner of the field. Here again two stiles with a bridge between them take you into another field. Carry on along the same line to the left-hand hedge and cross yet another stile. Continue diagonally along the enclosed track to the far right-hand corner where there is yet another stile. Go over this and follow the path across the field until you reach a stile where the path, after crossing over, turns sharp left. In front of you the ground falls steeply away and here, at Beaumont Chase, you can see Wardley Woods across the valley.

Looking over Beaumont Chase.

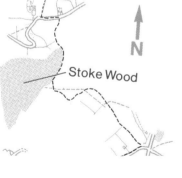

	Total Miles	Distance
Uppingham to Stoke Dry	3	3
Stoke Dry to Lyddington	3¹/₂	6¹/₂
Lyddington to Seaton	2¹/₂	9
Seaton to Morcott	2	11
Morcott to Barrowden	1³/₄	12³/₄

Leave Uppingham by the Stockerston Road. About fifty yards after passing the 30 MPH limit signs take the footpath on

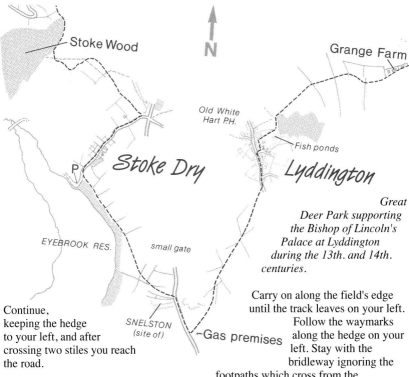

Stoke Wood

Grange Farm

N

Old White
Hart P.H.

Fish ponds

P

Stoke Dry

Lyddington

EYEBROOK RES.

small gate

*Great
Deer Park supporting
the Bishop of Lincoln's
Palace at Lyddington
during the 13th. and 14th.
centuries.*

SNELSTON
(site of)

Gas premises

Continue,
keeping the hedge
to your left, and after
crossing two stiles you reach
the road.

Carry on along the field's edge
until the track leaves on your left.
Follow the waymarks
along the hedge on your
left. Stay with the
bridleway ignoring the
footpaths which cross from the
hedgerow on the left shortly after you
enter the field and again by the gateway
as you leave it. Continue now with the
hedge on your right along the top of the
hill, finishing through stock-loading pens
onto the road. Turn right down the road
to Stoke Dry, passing the church of St.
Andrews on the left.

Turn left along the road for about two-
hundred yards until you find a bridleway
on the right. Take this, later passing the
entrance to Stoke Wood. Follow the
waymarks round the wood. As you leave
the wood continue on the bridleway
ignoring the path that crosses from the
field on the left into the woodland.

*As you leave the wood you have
excellent views of the Eyebrook
Reservoir, opened in 1940 to supply
water for Corby steelworks. The RAF's
617 squadron practised for the Moehne
Dam raid over these waters in 1943. The
land to the NE of you formed part of the*

*The hamlet of Stoke Dry has an
exceptionally interesting church with
architecture representing all the Gothic
styles. The Digby family made Stoke Dry
their principal seat in the 15th. century
and there are three interesting Digby
tombs. Note the 15th. century rood
screen across the Norman archway to
the chancel and the medieval murals in
the south (Chantry) chapel. There is no
truth in the rumour that part of the
Gunpowder Plot was hatched in the
small room above the north porch -
though Everard Digby was hanged for
his part in the plot in 1605.*

Across the Eyebrook Reservoir.   R.Adams

Continue on down the road. On the left, just before the fence round the Eyebrook Reservoir there is a bridleway. Follow this, keeping the Eyebrook enclosure perimeter on your right, passing through the first field and on along a grassy track. Then into the next field keeping the hedge on your right. You now enter another grassy track. Follow this ignoring the gate into the Eyebrook Reservoir enclosure, but aim for the field-gate ahead. Enter the field and take the path rising to the top right-hand corner on the horizon. It is worth looking back at the reservoir from this point. Follow the waymarks through the small gate opposite. The path goes right then shortly turns left down the middle of the field to reach the A6003 Uppingham/Caldecott road. There are views across the Welland Valley.

As you descend to the A6003 Seaton Viaduct can be seen ahead in the far distance and the site of the medieval village of Snelston lies just to the south of the track. It was a victim of the 16th

Seaton Viaduct.

Century wool enclosures: all that remains are discernible street and house positions and a fine circular windmill site.

Turn right along the A6003 and in about a third of a mile turn left into the tarmac drive leading to a gas pressure control station. (The grass verge on the western side of the road is wide for the whole length of this road-side stretch and it is recommended that it is used by walkers travelling in either direction alongside this busy road) From this point on the road you can see the yellow waymark post over the field that you are about to

cross (it will disappear from view as you go down the slope to the stile). Cross the stile at the end of the tarmac, cross the field, over another stile and another field. Now cross the third stile keeping to the right-hand hedge until you reach yet another stile. Cross this and a footbridge into the next field. Here you cut diagonally across the corner of the field to find a way into the next field. The path goes straight across this field to a stile. Cross this and, keeping the hedge on your left, after about 20 yds., over yet one more stile head diagonally right, aiming for the left of the farm buildings in the distance. You will approach a fence alongside a stream and cross over a bridge and through a gateway. When you reach the buildings follow the waymarks through them finishing over two stiles onto the road. On reaching the road turn left into Lyddington. By the Bishop's Eye, a tower set on the corner of the wall, turn right into Church Lane and go to the church.

Lyddington is full of attractive domestic buildings in ochre coloured ironstone and limestone. Take time to visit the lofty, perpendicular church - its nave and aisles have great beauty. There is a 15th, century rood screen, also medieval wall paintings and well preserved Laudian altar rails from 1635. Some interesting 15th. century brasses are hidden beneath the carpet in front of the altar. The Bede House, alongside the

The Bede House, Lyddington.   R.Adam

church, was originally a Palace belonging to the Bishops of Lincoln who would stay there with extensive retinues conducting business before moving on through their huge diocese. At the Reformation the buildings passed into lay hands and then to William Cecil, Lord Burleigh, who created a Hospital or Bede House out of it for 12 poor men, 2 women and a warden. It closed only in 1930.

Leave the church by the covered passage to the left which takes you past the Bede House and on to the Green.

Across the Green, on the main road, is the Olde White Hart.

Turn right and follow the track going past "Stoneleigh", the last house on the right on your way out of the Green. Here you will find a stile. Follow the waymarked path along the left-hand hedge until you come to a gateway on the left.

As you pass through these fields you will notice an elaborate number of rectangular trenches. These are remnants of the stew or fish ponds to supply the needs of the Bishop's followers and servants in the days when fresh fish was at a premium.

Turn into this gateway and continue along a very narrow field. In the left-hand corner cross a stile onto a track. Turn right up this track and take the waymarked path over the stile by the gateway straight ahead up the hill with woodland on your right. At the top of the hill cross the stile by a gate and continue, hedge on left, to the end of the field. Here turn right and in about 30 yds. turn

Near Grange Farm, approaching Seaton.

left to walk with a ditch on your left until you join the farm track by Grange Farm.

As you walk up from the farm you get a distant view of Seaton viaduct as it crosses the Welland valley to your right.

Continue up the track, turn right and walk through Seaton. You will pass the church and the George and Dragon public house.

Seaton has spacious views over the Welland Valley to the south and is strung out along the ridge. The church is worth a visit for its 12th. century chancel arch. Major-General Robert Overton - one of Cromwell's army commanders - is buried in the churchyard though no gravestone survives.

Seaton Viaduct.

R.Adams

To your right, after the crossroads, you will see the Seaton Railway Viaduct crossing the Welland Valley. This striking feature is 70ft. high and has 82 arches. It was built between 1876-1878 by some 3,000 navvies at a cost of £82,000. It has been calculated that 20 million bricks were made on site from local clay. For some years the line has only carried goods traffic but has recently been upgraded and now a daily passenger train to London from Oakham crosses the viaduct.

Carry straight on over the crossroads and in just over half a mile, at a bend in the road, a path leaves on the left.
Start by climbing the stile then cross diagonally right and over the stile to the next field. **Do not take the stile in the fence opposite which leads onto the railway track.** Turn left and follow the waymarks to the disused railway at the bottom of the field.

This is the old Uppingham branch-line.

Go under the culvert, cross the stile, and continue on a slightly left diagonal to cross a bridge. Now go directly ahead over the field in front to reach the hedgerow. Follow the path, hedge on right, through this field and two more.

Here take the waymarked path diagonally to your left, aiming just left of the electricity pole to the left of the houses on the horizon. When you reach the A47 on the top of the hill cross the main road and take the road opposite towards the village of Morcott. Immediately on the right is a stile. Take the path, aiming for the stile in the lefthand hedge. Over this go between the hawthorn bushes towards the electricity pole to the left of the house in front. Continue down this field and, at the stile, go down Mount Pleasant Road turning right along Morcott High Street to reach the White Horse Inn.

A short diversion left in this attractive village will take you to the Church of St. Mary the Virgin.

The church has many Norman relics including rich decoration in the north arcade. The south aisle has early English features.

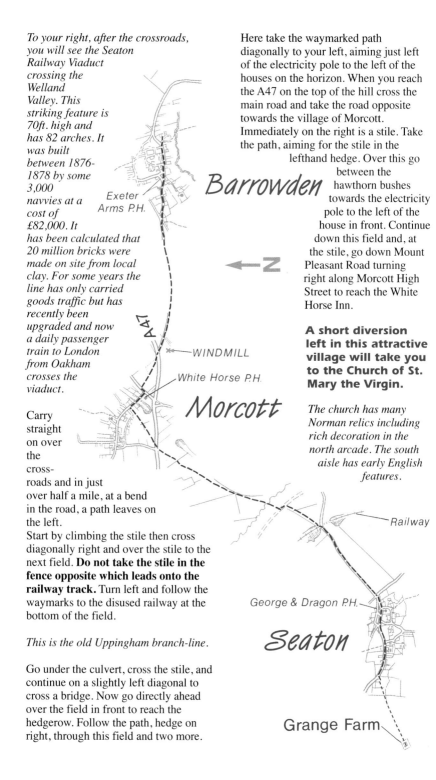

Barrowden

Exeter Arms P.H.

WINDMILL

White Horse P.H.

Morcott

Railway

George & Dragon P.H.

Seaton

Grange Farm

The Church is regularly open during the day. The large Morcott Hall was built in 1687 and has been a girls' boarding school for almost 50 years in the 20th. century, closing in 1989. At one time the village had five public houses but only the White Horse remains.

At the White Horse cross the road and take the path into the field opposite. Continue through the wooded area and at the far end of this cross the A47 and take the road by the windmill down to Barrowden, entering the village and continuing on to reach the Exeter Arms public house on your left.

The Morcott windmill has been rebuilt from a truncated tower into a dummy mill which is now a self-catering holiday cottage. Barrowden is a village with much good Elizabethan building in grey oolitic limestone, notably the Durant house (C1580) on The Green. The thatched large stone house to the east of the green is a recent construction. It was a royal manor at the time of Domesday and an important site in the Welland valley for the economic development of the area. It had a weekly market up to the time of the Black Death in 1349. Nowadays its pub, the Exeter Arms, and duck pond feature in many paintings and photographs. The church has a very fine 14th. century tower and broach spire and a beautiful 1588 Renaissance monument in the north aisle.

Exeter Arms and pond at Barrowden.   R.Adams

Morcott Windmill

Normanton Church.   *R.Adams*

BARROWDEN to EMPINGHAM

From Barrowden the route goes to the County boundary at the Wakerley Bridge, then on to Tixover keeping near the River Welland. From Tixover, via Tixover Grange to Geeston. Then on to Ketton, Normanton and into Empingham.

	Miles	Total Distance
Barrowden to Tixover	3	3
Tixover to Tixover Grange	1¼	4¼
Tixover Grange to Geeston	2	6¼
Geeston to Ketton	½	6¾
Ketton to Normanton	3¾	10½
Normanton to Empingham	2¾	13¼

Cross over the Green from the Exeter Arms and go down to the pavement opposite. Turn left and walking eastwards away from the pond keep on the pavement. Eventually, when you reach the next small Green bear right into Mill Lane. Here are two footpaths

Ignore the "Jurassic Way" which goes straight ahead down the steep path and soon crosses the river.

Take the path to the left over a stile. Follow the waymarks round a number of corners and across a small paddock, leaving by a kissing gate. Continue on to the far left corner of the fence ahead. Carry on along the same line and cross a plank bridge, then on to join the road by the bridge over the Welland.

Turn left, away from the river, and go about 1/4 mile along the road to find a bridleway on the right. Carry on along this with the hedge on your left until you reach the river. Here you go through the hedge and, with the hedge on your right, follow the river. Pass into the next field and on to a gate into the following field. Here keep to the top of the slope above the river and leave through the small gate into the wood. Follow the track through the wood, Welland Spinney. Leave the wood by the gate and follow the path, hedge on right, until you meet a stony track. Turn left along this and continue through to its end at Manor Farm. A track to Tixover church is on the right just as your way swings left and approaches the farm.

Exeter Arms P.H.

Barrowden

N➡

R. Welland

Welland Spinney

Tixover

TIXOVER GRANGE

R. Welland

Geeston

Duddington

Should you decide to make the short detour to the church you may wish to visit the village first where the key is available. A finger-post sign directs you to the house where it may be acquired.

The Parish Church of St. Luke's is close by the River Welland. It has a bold, chunky Norman tower and high clerestory nave. The manor of Tixover was given by the Bishop of Lincoln to the French Abbey of Cluny in 1130 and much of the church built between 1200 and 1230 was possibly Cluniac work There must have been some settlement - perhaps even a small village - around this church in earlier times. Roman remains have been unearthed and there are crop marks and signs of enclosures. Some evidence of piles in the Welland to the South suggests that there was once a bridge.

Pass through the farmyard and onto the road. Continue through the village keeping right along in front of the houses as you approach the main road. Do not carry on straight ahead to the road junction with the A47.

At the last house, having turned the corner, the road stops and a footpath continues. This then runs for some short distance alongside the A47 road. Keep to the path as it leaves the main road and then joins the road into Duddington. Carry on along this until you reach the start of the old bridge at Duddington. Here cross over the stile on the left and take the footpath which is also the Jurassic Way alongside the river to Tixover Grange. You pass under the A47 and continue along the river's edge until you reach a patch of willow trees. Here you can go straight ahead towards the opposite hedgerow where the waymarker can be seen up a short slope.
Alternatively you can keep alongside the river until you are opposite the waymark. Cross over the stile and turn right, keeping the fence on your right, until you come to a gate in this fence. Turn left, away from it, and cross over the stile now in front of you. Head across the field for the opposite hedge just right of the halfway point to find a stile leading onto the road. Turn right up the road. Just past the driveway into Tixover Grange take the fieldpath over a stile on the left. This goes diagonally right across the field. A stile takes you back onto the road.

The Old Bridge at Duddington.   R.Adams

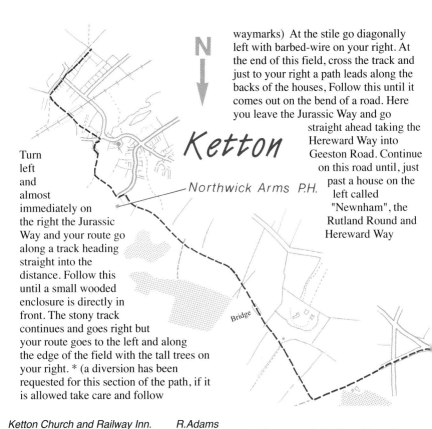

waymarks) At the stile go diagonally left with barbed-wire on your right. At the end of this field, cross the track and just to your right a path leads along the backs of the houses, Follow this until it comes out on the bend of a road. Here you leave the Jurassic Way and go straight ahead taking the Hereward Way into Geeston Road. Continue on this road until, just past a house on the left called "Newnham", the Rutland Round and Hereward Way

Ketton

Northwick Arms P.H.

Turn left and almost immediately on the right the Jurassic Way and your route go along a track heading straight into the distance. Follow this until a small wooded enclosure is directly in front. The stony track continues and goes right but your route goes to the left and along the edge of the field with the tall trees on your right. * (a diversion has been requested for this section of the path, if it is allowed take care and follow

Bridge

Ketton Church and Railway Inn.   R.Adams

turn left up a track. Follow this and cross the railway line by a footbridge. The path continues along a narrow alley going down steps to a road. Cross this and find a footpath between the houses opposite. The path opens out after it passes between two houses. Carry on along the hedge to a gap leading on to a road. Turn right here and follow the road keeping left at all junctions until you come to the end of the tarmac. Here you take the path over the bridge crossing the River Chater and continue straight ahead to pass the Methodist Chapel on your right. Following the path round by this, and then turning left up Bull Lane, you reach the main road through Ketton. To the left, about 100yds. away on the right-hand side of the road is the path to take out of Ketton.

To your right you can just see the "Northwick Arms".

Ketton quarry - path crossing the haul road

Entering Ketton from the SE as you have done gives you an unusual introduction to this very attractive village, with its practical domestic building in butter-coloured stone (interestingly not Ketton but Barnack stone). For sheer beauty the tower and spire of the church, glimpses of which can be seen on your left as you come up from the Chater to the village centre, is one of the best in the county. As you walk down the High Street notice the house next to the Post Office on the north side, which was given to Ketton by Belgian refugees who had been there during the First World War. Its plaque had the word KETTON deleted as a precaution against German invaders in 1940.

Follow the waymarks through the farmyard continuing on the track. As you reach the top of the rise it is worth stopping and looking back at the view. Carry on over the summit and continue on an embankment through the quarry crossing the haul-road on an impressive bridge. From this point follow the waymarked route on a changing diversion. Eventually, by 2012, the path will go directly from the bridge to the stile at the quarry boundary

Hanson (The Castle Cement Company) with its huge complex to the East of the village is one of Rutland's larger industrial concerns. Just to the east of the track on the embankment in 1998 Anglo-Saxon remains were found and the site was recorded by archaeologists before quarrying could take place. (square 9605)

Your path goes over the stile. Now go diagonally right to the right-hand hedge. Follow the hedge for a short distance until you reach the bridleway which crosses the path. Turn left along the bridleway crossing the field to reach a gateway. Here you join a track which enters an area with farm buildings and a house to the right (New Wood Lodge). Go through this and follow the track to the road. Ahead are views of RAF North Luffenham, now occupied by the army and re-named St. George's Barracks. Cross straight over and take the road ahead. In about 200 yds at the junction turn right and continue along the road. In just under a mile you pass a turning on the right to Normanton. Carry on, in about half a mile passing the stone built Oak Farm on the left. In front now you can see Rutland Water. At the T junction turn left towards Edith Weston and, in about 100 yds. turn right into the carpark for Rutland Water.

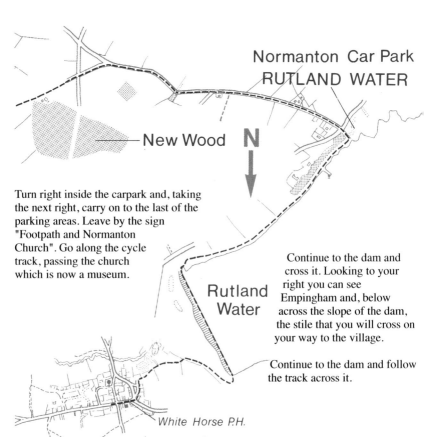

Normanton Car Park
RUTLAND WATER

New Wood

N

Turn right inside the carpark and, taking the next right, carry on to the last of the parking areas. Leave by the sign "Footpath and Normanton Church". Go along the cycle track, passing the church which is now a museum.

Rutland Water

Continue to the dam and cross it. Looking to your right you can see Empingham and, below across the slope of the dam, the stile that you will cross on your way to the village.

Continue to the dam and follow the track across it.

White Horse P.H.

Empingham

Rutland Water.   R.Adams

The Dam, completed in 1977, stands at the eastern end of Rutland Water. The reservoir's perimeter measures 24 miles and its waters reach a depth of 110 feet. The dam itself is 1200 metres long. It is constructed of Upper Lias Clay obtained from the flooded land. Several important archaeological finds were made before or during construction including Anglo-Saxon burial grounds yielding skeletons, grave jewellery and other artefacts as well as two Romano-British agricultural sites. At the northern end of the dam is the Sykes Lane car park, where 135 graves of Anglo-Saxon date were discovered. This large picnic area now has an Aquatic Centre. From the dam, if you look SW along the shore line, you can see Normanton Church (rebuilt in 1826), saved from the water by a coffer dam with a bank and causeway to give access. Today it is a museum devoted to the history of the reservoir.

Over the dam, staying inside the field, turn right and, with the fence on your left continue for some distance until you reach a stile by a gate (not either of the cycle gates but a fieldgate well down the fence) Go over this and cross diagonally over the field to the far corner. Here you will find a stile which leads into the wood. Take the path through the woodland, at its end following the steps down to a plank bridge and stile. Over this continue along the left-hand fence to the next stile. Cross over this then make your way diagonally right to the stile which is towards the left-hand end of the houses in front. Take the path between the houses to the road, "Nook Lane". Turn left along the lane and come to The White Horse public house across the main road in front of you.

Audit Hall, Empingham.

Empingham Village Green.

Norman Chancel Arch in Tickencote Church.

EMPINGHAM to THISTLETON

From Empingham the route passes through Tickencote, Great Casterton, Pickworth and on through quarries to Clipsham. From here it continues to Stretton and Thistleton passing close to the runway of RAF. Cottesmore.

	Miles	Total Distance
Empingham to Tickencote	3	3
Tickencote to Great Casterton	¹/₂	3¹/₂
Great Casterton to Pickworth	3	6¹/₂
Pickworth to Clipsham	2¹/₂	9
Clipsham to Stretton	1¹/₂	10¹/₂
Stretton to Thistleton	3	13¹/₂

Leave the "White Horse" and continue along the wide "Main Street" towards the Great North Road.

A very short diversion right at the cross-roads takes you to the Parish Church of St. Peter's.

From the cross-roads continue on along the Main Street, passing completely through the village and past the speed limit signs. On the right your track leads up through trees. As it leaves the woodland keep straight ahead. Pausing here to look behind you, you will see a view of Empingham. When you reach the concrete road bear right along it and keep on it until it turns sharp right. Here you carry straight on along the stony track. Carry on ahead along the track to the yellow waymark post at the end of the hedge in front. When the track enters the field keep the hedge on your left all the way to the spinney. Enter the spinney and keep to the track near the left-hand, northern, edge ignoring the strong track to the right. Leave the woodland and continue along the field-edge with the hedge on your left to the waymarker post. You take the right-hand track turning diagonally (at about 30 degrees to the hedgerow to go due east) across the field towards the two trees in the corner of the field. Join the concrete track and continue on past the plantation.

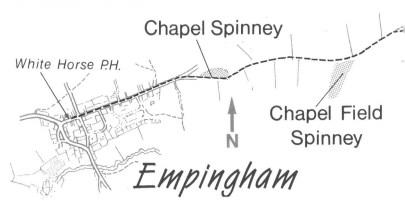

Chapel Spinney

White Horse P.H.

Chapel Field Spinney

N

Empingham

The church is well proportioned and has a fine tower and west front. It is largely 13th. century internally but later a porch, clerestory and many l 5th. century windows were added. Empingham was an important village in the Middle Ages with its weekly market. Note the Audit Hall (now local Village Hall) where the estate tenants paid their dues to the Lord of the Manor.

At the T junction turn right and take the path over the stile on the left. This goes diagonally right to the waymark post in the opposite corner of the field. Cross over the stile and go straight ahead, past the house on the left, along the concrete road. When this turns left carry on straight ahead along the field track. Cross over the stile and go diagonally slightly right to the waymark post.

Here go over the stile, cross the drive and over the stile opposite. The path goes straight ahead to the trees in front. Cross over the stile and make your way to the road. Turn right and go past Tickencote church.

A feature of this church is the magnificent Norman chancel-arch built between 1130 and 1150. The arch has six semi-circular orders and is immensely heavy. The sex partite vaulting in the chancel is remarkable. Much of the church was rebuilt in 1792 in keeping with its original Norman architecture.

Carry on straight ahead through the village taking the gate in the left-hand corner at the end of the street. Cross over the field to the stile onto the road opposite

Danish attacks in the period 867-76). Great Casterton has some attractive buildings as well as a 13th. -15th. century church.

Woodhead

Woodhead Castle - site of

Go past the "Plough" public house on your left and take the narrow road to the left just past the school road-sign. At the top of this, opposite the primary school, turn left and take the road towards Pickworth. Just over a mile along this road take the bridleway to

N

Tickencote

O K Diner

The Plough PH

Gt. Casterton

the "O.K. DINER" and the A1 service station.

Turn right and follow the road round, under the A1 into Great Casterton.

Great Casterton, on the old Great North Road where Ermine Street crossed the River Gwash, is now mercifully by-passed by the noisy A1. The village takes its name from the 1st. century castrum or Roman Fort to its NE which acquired urban status in the 2nd. - 5th. centuries. It had a late 4th. century villa where a hoard of coins was found hidden in its bath-house (probably buried against

the left. At the end of the first very large field on the right, after passing three ash trees in the right-hand hedge, turn right along a wide grassy track between two hedgerows. Follow this track. Continue straight ahead ignoring tracks off to right and left and keeping the field-boundary on your right for some distance until you come to a low point where a broad stony track crosses. Here you cross into the right-hand field and follow a grassy path up to a bridle gate. Go through this and carry on to another bridle gate. Through this gate the path goes straight across the field in front to a gap in the hedge. Through the gap take the left-hand hedge of the field and continue to the gateway into the final field of this track.

Bridleway to Pickworth.

Here, with the hedge on your right, you make your way to the road at Pickworth.

Pickworth is a good example of a deserted village. In the 13th. and early 14th. centuries it was quite large but by 1491 it was without inhabitants. Only one arch of the medieval church, which formed the south porch, remains. John Clare (born 1796), 'the ploughman's poet; worked as a day labourer, hedge setter and limekiln burner here. His wife, 'Sweet Patty of the Vale', was a Great Casterton girl. He was deeply attached

to rural life and landscape and between 1821 and 1835 published three successful volumes of poetry, autobiographical letters and prose. Later, sadly, he became mentally disturbed, was certified insane and spent the rest of his life in Northampton General Asylum where he continued to write disturbingly and with a deep sense of personal loss.

Opposite in front of the Church is a heritage board with historic facts about the village. Unfortunatly the John Clare Kiln is now sited on private land and can no longer be visited

Turn left and continue along the road, going past the bridleway on the right just past Manor Farm. Now, leaving the village behind you, take the next bridleway on the right. Follow this through two fields. At the gateway take the waymarked bridleway diagonally right towards the wood, heading just left of the centre of the woodland. Enter the wood by a bridle gate and follow the path in the wood. When the path leaves the wood follow the waymarks carefully as the route may change as quarrying continues. You will enter the quarry in the far right corner of the field at the edge of the woodland

Quarrying has been carried out here, south of the village of Clipsham, since the 13th. century. Stone from here has gone to many well known buildings such as Peterborough and Ely Cathedrals, Oxford Colleges, Burley-on-the-Hill and, after World War II, to rebuild the House of Commons, bombed in 1941. Today the product is mainly roadstone.

Lime Kiln – John Clare site, Pickworth.   G.Dunn

Clipsham

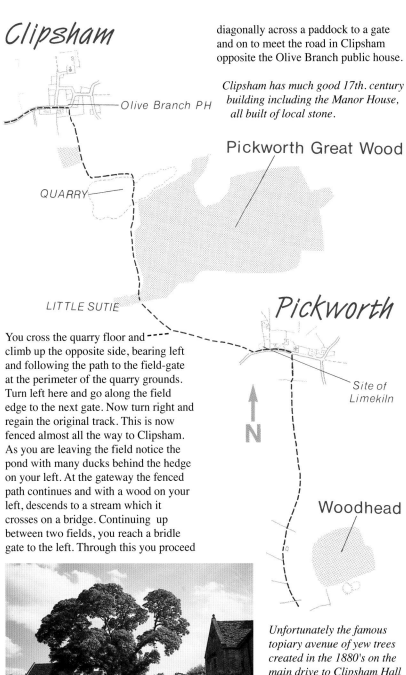

Olive Branch PH

QUARRY

LITTLE SUTIE

Pickworth Great Wood

Pickworth

Site of
Limekiln

↑
N

Woodhead

diagonally across a paddock to a gate
and on to meet the road in Clipsham
opposite the Olive Branch public house.

*Clipsham has much good 17th. century
building including the Manor House,
all built of local stone.*

You cross the quarry floor and
climb up the opposite side, bearing left
and following the path to the field-gate
at the perimeter of the quarry grounds.
Turn left here and go along the field
edge to the next gate. Now turn right and
regain the original track. This is now
fenced almost all the way to Clipsham.
As you are leaving the field notice the
pond with many ducks behind the hedge
on your left. At the gateway the fenced
path continues and with a wood on your
left, descends to a stream which it
crosses on a bridge. Continuing up
between two fields, you reach a bridle
gate to the left. Through this you proceed

A corner of Clipsham.   R.Adams

*Unfortunately the famous
topiary avenue of yew trees
created in the 1880's on the
main drive to Clipsham Hall
lies a good mile along the
Castle Bytham road. Too far
for most walkers who intend
to complete the journey to
Thistleton.*

Turn left taking the road to Stretton. The Woodland Trust has acquired land on the North side of this road from a point where a bridleway leaves and on towards Stretton, The Rutland Round now leaves the road and follows the grass track

and take the path over the stile opposite. This leads diagonally to a farmtrack. Turn left along this and shortly join the Viking Way. Turn right on this and continue until the hedge stops. Here you go straight ahead across the field in front aiming in the direction of the tall aerial on the horizon. You cross the flight-path for R.A.F. Cottesmore passing by the wooden fencing protecting the approach lights.

Cottesmore opened in 1938 and was home to USAAF for part of World War Two. Recently it was

Thistleton

N

Hooby Lodge

R.A.F. COTTESMORE AIRFIELD

A1

The Jackson Stops P

inside the hedge until the outskirts of Stretton. The route lies straight on to the Al passing under it and on to the roundabout ahead.

By diverting through Stretton village you will find the "Jackson Stops" public house and the church.

At the roundabout on the west side of the A1 take the footpath which leaves the northbound slip-road over a plank bridge and stile. Follow this across the field crossing a concrete track and on over a footbridge and another field to meet the road. Here turn right and, at the bend in the road, take the footpath on the right diagonally across the field to a bridge over a ditch. Turn left along the hedgerow and right at the waymark to reach the road at a stile. Cross the road

Stretton

a Tornado base and the Tri-National Training Establishment for pilots from the forces of Britain, Germany and Italy. It is now a Harrier base but is threatened with closure in 2014.

At the last of the approach lights carry on to the small gap in the hedge ahead. There is a waymark post on the left-hand side of the gap but it is often lost from sight in the hedge. Cross the next field going down and then up the opposite slope heading for the waymark which is directly in line with the aerial in the distance. From this point the path goes straight over to the opposite hedgerow as waymarked. Here turn left and with the hedge on your right continue until leaving the field and reaching the Thistleton main street where the route continues to the left.

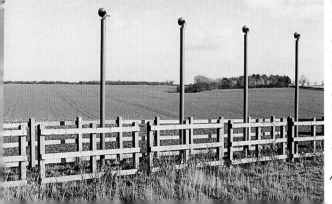

Approach lights. G.Dunn

Passageway to Oakham market place.

THISTLETON to OAKHAM

Leaving Thistleton by the Sewstern Road the route follows the County Boundary running along a ridge giving good views, particularly on the Rutland side. This continues to Teigh. (pronounced TEE) Here a footpath opposite the church takes you to join the bridleway to Whissendine. From here you continue to Langham and then, via the high ground above it, into Barleythorpe and on to Oakham.

	Miles	Total Distance
Thistleton to Teigh	4½	4½
Teigh to Whissendine	2½	7
Whissendine to Langham	2	9
Langham to Barleythorpe	2½	11½
Barleythorpe to Oakham	1¼	12¾

There is little of note in Thistleton.

Its medieval church has been rebuilt twice. Go round the back to see how close it is to the old Rectory. White Horse Cottage was once an Inn.

INDUSTRIAL ESTATE

Barns

Thistleton

N

Thistleton Gap, G.Dunn

At Thistleton follow the road westwards. Pass by the left turn to Market Overton and take the Sewstern road. This turns sharp right and continues in a northerly direction. In the distance, on the left of the road two large barns can be seen. Carry on along the road until you reach the gate that leads in to them.

On the opposite side of the road is Thistleton Gap. This is the site of bare-knuckle fights, hugely popular but illegal. Being at the meeting place of three counties, Leicestershire, Lincolnshire and Rutland there was a convenient escape route should any magistrate appear. On 28th. September 1811 Tom Cribb beat an American, Thomas Molyneux in the Heavyweight Boxing Championship of the World. Many prints were subsequently made of this occasion. It is reported there was a crowd of 15,000 for this event.

A bridleway goes through the gates and across in front of the barns. At the end of the further (Dutch) barn the track goes diagonally right across the field to the corner of the hedge. Continue along the edge of the field with the hedge on your right. At the corner of the field go through the gap in the hedge in front of you and turn right. Keeping the hedge on your right, go into the corner of the field, follow round to the left and on to the next right-hand corner. Still with the hedge on your right, proceed to the corner of the field and turn left, still keeping the hedge on your right. As you continue along this field hedge you will see a house over the hedge to your right.

This is Cribb's Lodge, no doubt connected with the Prize-fighter. Some say it was his training base.

Woodwell Head—

IN D
ES

About 100 yds. before the corner of the field there is a stile on the right. Do not cross it. Your path goes on to the corner and then turns left, keeping the hedge on your right until you reach the end of

Dis. Canal—

Indistinct paths to Market Overton

N

Teigh

"Thomas" carved on it, has been placed in the hedge on your left giving a resting place with views across to Market Overton. Go on past this. Further on there is once again just a hedge on the right. A footpath from Market Overton to Edmondthorpe crosses your path. The main track, which is your way, turns left at a point where a bridleway is waymarked straight ahead. At the end of this field is a gate. Go through the gate and follow the track over the route of the old canal

the hedge where the bridleway joins a farm track coming from behind you on the right. Continue on this track to the corner in front of you and go round to the right. Carry on along the track with the hedge on your right. Shortly a bridleway leaves to the left, going through an industrial estate and on to Market Overton. Your route continues along the track ahead with the hedge still on the right. After about 1/2 mile the hedge encloses woodland. Shortly your path turns left to remain on the edge of the wood. (**A bridleway goes on straight into the wood at this point. Do not take it**) Carry on along the path with the wood on your right. You reach a corner where a waymark shows a path directly ahead.

Turn right and continue along the edge of the wood. Soon the track is enclosed on both sides. The wood stops. Shortly a bridleway joins from the left. As you go down the slope a seat, with the name

This was part of the Melton to Oakham canal, opened in December 1802. It was closed by 1848 after the coming of the railway which took all the trade.

Then, passing the hawthorn bushes and raised grass bank, bear right and go towards a gate in the right-hand hedge. Aim for the tree to the right of both the single electricity pole and the house on the horizon. This leads on to a track which takes you to a road. Turn left here and follow the road into Teigh. Pass the road to the right to Whissendine and, after the Teigh sign, take a right turn into the village eventually reaching the church.

Holy Trinity, Teigh, is a gem of a rebuilt 18th. century church whose interior is almost entirely intact. The rebuilding was undertaken at his own expense, in 1782, by the rector, the Revd. Robert Sherard, who served there for forty

Teigh Church from the footpath to the West, G.Dunn

opposite hedge. This takes you onto a bridleway. Turn right and shortly cross the railway-line. Just along the bridleway a footpath leaves to the left. Ten years ago when the Rutland Round was devised this path was not clear on the ground and it would have been unwise to use it. It now provides a pleasant, more elevated route and is a recommended alternative except in wet weather when its crossfield paths could be very muddy. Directions for this route can be found at the end of this section, or follow this bridleway to its end in about 1 ¼ miles. Here, on the outskirts of Whissendine, turn left along the road. In about 200 yds.

years. He later succeeded to his family seat as Earl of Harborough and built a similar church on his inherited estate at Stapleford Park The pews are arranged in tiers facing each other in collegiate style. The pulpit, lectern and prayer desks are at the west end. All is light and colourful and well worth a visit.

Leave Teigh by the path over the road opposite the west end of the church. Go straight across the field heading for an electricity pole, the top of which can be seen from ' the stile. As you approach the fence you will see a stile just to your right. By taking this route you should have avoided having to cross a boggy patch. Once over the stile make for the right-hand hedge and the far right-hand corner. Here go through the gate in front and the take the bridge immediately on your right. Then turn left, and with the hedge on your left continue until you reach a long footbridge. Cross this and then go diagonally right to a gateway in the

Dis. Canal

N

Teigh

Railway

pass a footpath on the left. ** Opposite is a cemetery. At its end take the gate on your right and through this go diagonally left to the far corner. Here go over the stile and left to the churchyard wall. Cross the stile in the fence in front. From the stile, looking to your right, you can see the Whissendine windmill on the skyline.

Make your way over the cattle-grid along the drive to the road ahead. *The main part of Whissendine lies to the west of your route and its present-day shape is rather strung out with additional modern estates for commuters. It has a splendid church. Admire especially the perpendicular tower, the window tracery, the 15th. century nave roof and the 16th. century screen between the transept and the aisle which came in 1869 from St. John's College Cambridge, courtesy of Sir Giles Gilbert Scott.*

To the right, about 100 yds. down the road, is the Three Horseshoes public house. Further down the street, by the stream, is the White Lion, which at the time of writing is more likely to be open during weekday lunchtimes.

The route turns left and, in front of the church, you cross the road and go into the new housing estate opposite. Bear left up Foxhill. Keep on the left-hand path, ignoring the Close, and follow it when, at the end of the road, it goes along the side of No. 21. When you reach the field turn left. At the gateway onto the road the path turns right and follows the hedge for about 200 yds. joining the road at a stile. Turn right along the road and continue to a sharp left bend. Here you go straight ahead into a bridleway to Langham. Carry on with the hedge on your left. When the hedge changes to be on your right you are at the summit of the track.

It is worth stopping here and looking at the view in all directions. At the junction of bridleways at the end of the field turn right and continue with the hedge on your left. In the next field keep a good look out for a path leaving on the left just after a wide gap in the hedge. Take this and, with a deep ditch on your left, carry on straight ahead. Cross a plank bridge and continue until you reach a hedge blocking your way in front.. Turn right and, in about 150 yds., at a waymark turn left over a bridge. Go diagonally right to a waymark near a tree in the right-hand hedge. Turn left and, keeping the hedge on your right, continue to the end of the field. Here you go through the hedge in front and turn right following the right¬hand hedgerow round the field to the far right corner. Here a stile takes you onto Manor Lane, Langham.

Whissendine

THREE HORSESHOES P.H.

A606

THE NOEL ARMS P.H.

railway

N

Langham

Barleythorpe

A606

Railway Station

playing fields

Oakham

Langham has a complicated plan, basically a rectangular space which reveals its origin as a forest settlement. The church whose handsome spire can be seen over the rooftops to the left is mainly 13th. century with clerestory added later.

Oakham and Rutland Water from above Barleythorpe, R.Adams

Inside it is conspicuous for the amount of space and light which the use of much clear glass accentuates. Until recently Langham was the home of "Ruddles Beer" which achieved a nation-wide market in 1970's and 80's. The company has, however, been taken over - has changed hands several times - and the brewery site is now a housing estate.

From the stile turn right and then left into Orchard Road. At the bottom of Orchard Road turn right and then left into Bridge Street. When you have crossed the bridge turn right by the Noel Arms into Church Street. At the end of Church Street go straight over the main road to the footpath opposite. Follow the path between two hedges and on until it turns left and comes to a road. Cross the road and go right, very shortly taking the bridleway on the left signed "Braunston 3 Miles". Follow this keeping the hedge on your left along the field, through the gate in front into a track between the hedge and a post and wire fence. At the gate into the next field the path follows

the left-hand hedge and is waymarked. Follow this hedge to the wood at the top of the field then turn right and keep the wood on your left all the way to its end. Here you turn right and continue with the hedge on your left to the waymarked field gate. Go through the gate and cross the field ahead to reach another gate onto Manor Lane. This is probably the best viewpoint to pause at for views over Oakham and Rutland Water. Go left down Manor Lane to Barleythorpe. As you enter the village the road has two sharp bends. Follow it to the main road and turn right following the pavement alongside the main road for about a quarter of a mile. Before the sign for Oakham is reached there is a stile in the hedge on the right. At the time of writing you ignore this and follow the pavement to the roundabout.

Here you turn right into Huntsman's Drive. **Eventually, when the School is built, you will take the path over the stile and wind your way on a firm path between ornamental ponds then past the carpark to reach this point.**

On the left you will see the footpath sign and follow the path through the trees, back onto the path and down the side of the care village entering the main road opposite Oakham Station from Park Lane.

Oakham is now once again the County Town and centre of County Government from Catmose. The town is famous for its fine church of All Saints, its Elizabethan Grammar School now considerably expanded to a modern 1,000 strong, co-educational independent school, its Norman fortified manor house (Oakham Castle) where the famous "Horseshoe" collection is to be_ found and its County Museum, housed in the Old Riding School of the Rutland 'Fencibles' raised in 1794. It is also known for its signal-box alongside the level-crossing which is the prototype Hornby used for its model railways.

There is much to see in Oakham but if you are carrying straight on the suggested route is to cross the level-crossing, bear left and cross over the road to go along Northgate. This will bring you to the Parish Church of "All Saints". Take the passageway between the church and Oakham School Chapel. Go straight ahead coming into the Market Square via the Butter Cross, Post Office and Oakham Castle. Make your way to the High Street. Turn left and take Catmos Street, the road to Uppingham, passing by the Library and crossing the Stamford Road to reach the Offices of Rutland County Council. The Round completed you are once more back at Rutland County Museum. The route is now described in the Oakham to Uppingham section, section one.

Alternative Route into Whissendine

*Take the footpath to the left and cross diagonally towards a clump of trees on the far side of the field. Continue across the next field and when you reach the hedge follow it to your right to reach the corner. Through the hedge aim at the church tower in the distance and, at the bottom of the slope, you will find a way over a bridge through the hedge. Continue crossfield up the slope cross the drive and take the path through the allotments. You join the road opposite the cemetery. Turn left and then follow the directions from ***

The path through Clipsham Quarry, where the route may change as quarrying continues.

Clipsham Quarry.

View from Whissendine Church Tower showing the Rutland Round in the foreground just outside the churchyard wall. The Three Horseshoes public house is on the right about 100 yards down the road.   *R.Adams*

Campaign to Protect Rural England

3 ways to support CPRE

Please complete this form and return it to: Supporter Services, CPRE, Freepost SW3524, LONDON SE1 0YZ. No stamp is needed.

Mr/Mrs/Miss/Ms _____ Initials _____ Surname _____

Organisation _____

Address _____

_____ Postcode _____

Tel _____ / Email _____

1. BECOME A MEMBER

I would like to become a member.
(Join by Direct Debit and receive three months' membership free.)

	Recommended minimum	or your preferred amount
Individual	☐ £29.00	£ _____
Joint (two adults)	☐ £38.00	£ _____
Family	☐ £44.00	£ _____
Concessionary*	☐ £12.00	£ _____
Under 25	☐ £6.00	£ _____
Organisation	☐ £32.00	£ _____
Parish council	☐ £29.00	£ _____

* Includes those living on state pension, low income, income support or jobseekers' allowance.

You will also be a member of a CPRE county branch.

Please state county_____
(CPRE has a branch in every county and a branch that covers Greater London.)

I would like to receive a copy of the CPRE's constitution ☐
and/or my branch constitution ☐

2. GIVE A REGULAR GIFT

I wish to give CPRE a regular gift of £ _____ per month/quarter/year
Please fill in the Direct Debit and Gift Aid Declaration overleaf.

3. GIVE A DONATION

I would like to give a gift of £ _____.
Please fill in payment details below and Gift Aid Declaration overleaf.

PAYMENT

☐ I enclose a cheque/CAF voucher made payable to CPRE for £ _____
☐ I have completed the Direct Debit overleaf
☐ I wish to pay by Mastercard/Visa/American Express/CAFCard/Maestro

Please state total amount £ _____

Card No. ☐☐☐☐☐ ☐☐☐☐☐ ☐☐☐☐☐ ☐☐☐☐☐ ☐☐☐☐☐
Expiry date ☐☐/☐☐ Start date ☐☐/☐☐ or Maestro Issue No.____

Signature _____ **Date** _____

GET INVOLVED

Whether or not you decide to support CPRE financially, you can help us win vital campaigns.

☐ Please tick here if you would like to join our team of letter-writers
☐ Please tick here if you would like to receive our monthly campaigns email.
(Please make sure you complete your email address above.) **Thank you.**

BRANC/B/NL/ITTS/2009

Notes

Notes

Notes

Notes

Notes